RAND

Investigating Optimal Replacement of Aging Air Force Systems

Edward G. Keating, Matthew Dixon

Prepared for the
United States Air Force

Project AIR FORCE

The research reported here was sponsored by the United States Air Force under Contract F49642-01-C-0003. Further information may be obtained from the Strategic Planning Division, Directorate of Plans, Hq USAF.

Library of Congress Cataloging-in-Publication Data

Keating, Edward G. (Edward Geoffrey), 1965-
    Investigating optimal replacement of aging Air Force systems / Edward G. Keating, Matthew C. Dixon.
        p. cm.
    Includes bibliographical references.
    "MR-1763."
    ISBN 0-8330-3483-9 (pbk. : alk. paper)
    1. United States. Air Force—Procurement—Mathematical models. 2. KC–135 (Tanker aircraft) 3. Lear jet aircraft. 4. Jet transports—United States—Maintenance and repair—Mathematical models. I. Dixon, Matthew C. II. Title.

UG1123.K43223 2003
358.4'1621—dc22

2003020469

RAND is a nonprofit institution that helps improve policy and decisionmaking through research and analysis. RAND® is a registered trademark. RAND's publications do not necessarily reflect the opinions or policies of its research sponsors.

Published 2003 by RAND
1700 Main Street, P.O. Box 2138, Santa Monica, CA 90407-2138
1200 South Hayes Street, Arlington, VA 22202-5050
201 North Craig Street, Suite 202, Pittsburgh, PA 15213-1516
RAND URL: http://www.rand.org/
To order RAND documents or to obtain additional information, contact Distribution Services: Telephone: (310) 451-7002; Fax: (310) 451-6915; Email: order@rand.org

Preface

Whether to maintain or replace an aging system is a common decision. Anyone who owns an automobile, for instance, eventually grapples with this issue. At some point, it seems wrong to continue to repair an aging system. However, replacement systems typically entail considerable up-front investment.

This study continues a sequence of RAND Project AIR FORCE reports on aging aircraft and the replacement-repair decision, of which Greenfield and Persselin (2002) and Pyles (2003) are recent examples. The research took place in a project on "Aging Aircraft: Forecasting Capabilities and Costs." Here, we develop a parsimonious model of the repair-replacement decision and apply the model to the Air Force's C-21A transport and KC-135 tanker aircraft. The research reported here was sponsored by Brigadier General Elizabeth A. Harrell (AF/ILM) and Major General Ronald J. Bath (AF/XPX) and conducted within the Resource Management Program of RAND's Project AIR FORCE.

This research should be of interest to U.S. Air Force and other Department of Defense acquisition and logistics personnel.

Project AIR FORCE

Project AIR FORCE (PAF), a division of RAND, is the U.S. Air Force's federally funded research and development center for studies and analyses. PAF provides the Air Force with independent analyses of policy alternatives affecting the development, employment, combat readiness, and support of current and future aerospace forces. Research is performed in four programs: Aerospace Force Development; Manpower, Personnel, and Training; Resource Management; and Strategy and Doctrine.

Additional information about PAF is available on our web site at http://www.rand.org/paf.

Contents

Figures

Tables

Summary

This report examines a common problem: Whether to continue to repair an aging system or to invest in a new replacement. In particular, we look at this issue from the perspective of the United States Air Force.

Modeling the Decision to Repair or Replace an Aging Aircraft

We consider a type of aircraft (e.g., a tanker) that the Air Force envisions having in its inventory, in some form, into the foreseeable future. We then consider the decision to operate an existing aircraft for one more year or to replace it with a new version right now.

Operating an existing aircraft for one more year results in some aircraft availability level at the cost of the requisite maintenance, fuel, and labor. In contrast, purchasing a new aircraft results in a stream of both costs and aircraft availability.

We find that the Air Force should repair, rather than replace, an aging system if and only if the availability-adjusted marginal cost of the existing aircraft is less than the replacement's average cost per available year.

The C-21A Repair Versus Replacement Decision

We applied our methodology to the C-21A, the Air Force's version of the Learjet 35 passenger aircraft.

According to data provided to RAND by the C-21A program office, the aircraft has had variable, but generally increasing, maintenance and modification costs over time. Of particular concern to the C-21A program office is a major renovation of the aircraft set forth in its system and component replacement schedule for the 2012 timeframe.

We find, with our current parameter estimates, that it probably would be appropriate to undertake the replacement schedule's 2012 renovation, but that the C-21A should be retired sometime around 2020. (See pp. 11– 12.)

Estimating Model Parameters for the KC-135

We next applied our model to the KC-135 tanker.

The Air Force's KC-135 fleet is, on average, over 40 years old. The fleet has had considerable problems in recent years, including degraded availability and increased installation-level on- and off-equipment maintenance costs. The KC-135's programmed depot maintenance package has also grown.

We obtained KC-135 operating and support cost estimates from RAND colleague Michael Kennedy. Those cost estimates, in conjunction with our maintenance cost growth-rate estimates, were used to populate our model.

It is uncertain what would replace the KC-135, but for illustrative purposes we assumed a Boeing 767 replacement. We then made a series of assumptions about how 767 tanker maintenance costs and availability would evolve as the aircraft aged.

With the parameters we used, we find it will be optimal to replace the KC-135 before the end of the decade. This finding is broadly in accord with Kennedy et al.'s unpublished RAND research. We caution, however, that our parameter estimates are speculative; we urge more in-depth analysis of this issue. (See pp. 30–32.)

Acknowledgments

The authors appreciate the assistance, comments, and suggestions of RAND colleagues Carl Dahlman, Lionel Galway, Jean Gebman, Victoria Greenfield, Gregory Hildebrandt, Michael Kennedy, Robert Leonard, Daniel Norton, Raymond Pyles, Timothy Ramey, C. R. Roll, Jane Siegel, Fred Timson, and Alan Vick on this paper. Jeanne Heller edited this document and David Bolhuis provided administrative support. We received insightful reviews of an early draft from Professor Michael Alles of Rutgers University and Laura Baldwin of RAND. Dick Enz of Getronics Government Solutions helped with the Reliability and Maintainability Information System (REMIS). Section 3 was informed by helpful discussions with and information provided by Captain Charles Bolton of Air Mobility Command and Mike Cottrell, Peter Erickson, Dolores Hulsey, and Rod Mills of the Oklahoma City Air Logistics Center. Brent Boning and Peter Francis of the Center for Naval Analyses and David Frye and Terry Mitchell of Lockheed Martin Aeronautics also provided helpful assistance.

An earlier version of this research was presented to the 6th Joint FAA/DoD/NASA Conference on Aging Aircraft in San Francisco on September 18, 2002. We also benefited from comments of seminar audiences at Air Mobility Command Headquarters at Scott Air Force Base on February 10, 2003 and at the C-21A program office at Tinker Air Force Base on April 1, 2003. This research was briefed at the Western Economic Association Conference in Denver on July 14, 2003; Gary Bliss of the Office of the Secretary of Defense constructively discussed the research.

We also benefited from comments received at the United States Air Force Academy on July 28, 2003.

Of course, remaining errors are the authors' responsibility.

Abbreviations

AF/ILM	Headquarters, United States Air Force, Installations and Logistics, Directorate of Maintenance
AF/XPX	Headquarters, United States Air Force, Plans and Programs, Directorate of Strategic Planning
DoD	Department of Defense
FAA	Federal Aviation Administration
FMC	Fully Mission Capable
FY	Fiscal Year
NASA	National Aeronautics and Space Administration
OMB	Office of Management and Budget
PDM	Programmed Depot Maintenance
REMIS	Reliability and Maintainability Information System

1. Introduction

Whether to replace or repair an aging system is a common decision. For example, anyone who owns a car has to decide, at some point, whether to continue to repair the car or, fearing repairs would be "good money after bad," replace it. Replacing the vehicle would require up-front investment but would (it is hoped) lead to diminished repair requirements until the replacement vehicle itself faces impaired operation and increased maintenance cost.

There is a sizable literature on the repair versus replacement decision, some of which is discussed in Greenfield and Persselin (2002). Jondrow et al. (2001) developed a repair-replacement model for the U.S. Navy.

The United States Air Force faces similar issues with its aircraft. As we will show, evidence suggests that maintenance costs tend to increase as aircraft age whereas aircraft availability tends to decrease. Further, older aircraft may lack capabilities the Air Force wished they had. At the same time, new aircraft are expensive, so the Air Force cannot and does not blithely replace a system. RAND was asked to help the Air Force consider the tradeoff between continuing to maintain versus replacing an aging system.

This paper presents and implements a relatively simple model of how the Air Force could decide when to replace an aging system. Building on the work of Greenfield and Persselin (2002), Section 2 presents a relatively straightforward optimality condition. Specifically, it is shown to be optimal to continue to repair an aircraft if the annual cost of doing so is less than the annualized total cost of a new aircraft (controlling for aircraft availability levels).

We next illustrate usage of our approach. In Section 3, we examine the Air Force's C-21A transport jet. The C-21A program office initially proposed this research project to RAND, so it was sensible to apply our approach to C-21A data they provided. We find it would probably be appropriate to replace the C-21A around 2020.

In Section 4, we apply our methodology to the KC-135 tanker fleet. There is considerable controversy about the KC-135 and whether, when, and how it should be replaced. See, for instance, United States General Accounting Office (2002), Svitak and Kaufman (2003), Squeo and Lunsford (2003), and Graham (2003). Using data and assumptions about the KC-135's replacement provided by RAND colleague Michael Kennedy, we populate our model and find the KC-135 should be replaced by the end of the decade. We do not, however, consider the controversy on whether the Air Force should lease or buy a KC-135 replacement.

For both the C-21A and the KC-135 cases, our objective is not to come to a definitive conclusion on what the Air Force should do about these systems. Instead, we present an analytic methodology that could be applied across different weapon systems as part of more detailed analysis.

We focus on the case where an aircraft is being replaced by a new aircraft with similar capabilities. As a practical matter, the Air Force might wish to replace an old aircraft with a new aircraft that is faster, stealthier, or otherwise more desirable. We will discuss how our approach might be adapted to that case. To a first approximation, however, ours here is best suited to analysis of a case where an aging system is replaced by a new system with similar capabilities.

2. Modeling the Decision to Repair or Replace an Aging Aircraft

Modeling the Decision

We consider a type of aircraft (e.g., a tanker) that the Air Force envisions having in its inventory (in one form or another) into the foreseeable future. This string of future tankers would have a string of discounted future expenses

$$x = \sum_{t=1}^{\infty} \frac{Expend_{Rt}}{(1 + Discount)^{t-1}},$$

where the first replacement tanker (we use R to denote the replacement, rather than incumbent, aircraft) flew in Year 1 and $Discount$ was the Office of Management and Budget's prescribed real interest rate (currently 3.2 percent). As we will discuss, we assume the Air Force uses an algorithm to determine when to replace its tankers.

These future tankers will provide a string of available tanker days (or fractions of years). The Office of Management and Budget (OMB) Circular A-94 prescribes that "all future benefits and costs, including non-monetized benefits and costs, should be discounted." Hence, symmetric to x, we can define a future availability sum

$$y = \sum_{t=1}^{\infty} \frac{Availability_{Rt}}{(1 + Discount)^{t-1}}.$$

Consider, then, an existing incumbent aircraft, I. Without loss of generality, we will focus on the question of whether the Air Force should fly the incumbent aircraft one more year before replacing it or replace it right now. (There is no loss of generality in this simplification. If, for instance, it is in fact optimal to operate the incumbent aircraft for six more years, it will certainly be optimal to operate it for one more year.)

If the incumbent aircraft is kept only one more year, the Air Force spends $Expend_{I1}$ to sustain and operate the aircraft and receives fraction $Availability_{I1}$ years of availability (or $365 * Availability_{I1}$ days). $Expend_{I1}$ would include, for instance, the maintenance, fuel, and labor costs associated with flying the incumbent aircraft another year. Then, starting next year, the replacement's

4

strings of expenses and availability start. The replacement's expenses would include production, testing, and research and development costs not yet borne, as well as the operating costs of the aircraft. Therefore, the discounted infinite sum of expenditures associated with keeping the incumbent one more year would be

$$Expend_{I1} + \frac{x}{1 + Discount},$$

whereas the sum of availability would be

$$Availability_{I1} + \frac{y}{1 + Discount}.$$

(The Air Force still pays x to get y years of availability from the replacements, but it has been pushed back by one year and hence is discounted.)

Suppose the Air Force's sole goal is to minimize its expenditures. Then it would operate the existing aircraft another year if and only if

$$Expend_{I1} + \frac{x}{1 + Discount} \leq x \text{ or } Expend_{I1} \leq \frac{x * Discount}{1 + Discount}.$$

However, we do not think the Air Force's sole goal is expenditure minimization because this goal would not consider the availability of its aircraft. Instead, the Air Force's goal may be to minimize its average cost per available year (or day). With this metric, retaining the incumbent aircraft for one more year results in an average cost per available year of

$$\frac{Expend_{I1} + \dfrac{x}{1 + Discount}}{Availability_{I1} + \dfrac{y}{1 + Discount}}.$$

Therefore, the Air Force should repair, rather than replace, an aging system for one more year if and only if

$$\frac{Expend_{I1} + \dfrac{x}{1 + Discount}}{Availability_{I1} + \dfrac{y}{1 + Discount}} \leq \frac{x}{y} \text{ or } \frac{Expend_{I1}}{Availability_{I1}} \leq \frac{x}{y}.$$

For future notation, we denote the availability-adjusted marginal cost of the incumbent

$$MC_I = \frac{Expend_{I1}}{Availability_{I1}},$$

whereas

$$AC_R = \frac{x}{y}$$

equals the replacement's annualized cost per available year.

There are a number of assumptions underlying this $MC_I \leq AC_R$ optimality condition. The assumption that the Air Force's objective is to minimize its average cost per available aircraft year is one.

Another assumption is that MC_I is nondecreasing past its minimum (i.e., that once MC_I exceeds AC_R, it does not later fall below it). Fortunately, as we will demonstrate in Section 3, one can find the optimum when there are multiple crossings of MC_I and AC_R by simply comparing the different crossings' average costs per available year.

One might hope that replacement aircraft are retired optimally (i.e., AC_R is minimized). However, if we knew future replacement aircraft were not to be kept for optimal durations, AC_R would increase and one would hold on to the incumbent aircraft longer. In an illustration below, we show how the optimal retirement age N might be computed.

If one wished to apply this optimality condition in the real world, we would not recommend one wait until the optimal retirement year to take action because there are lags associated with acquiring a replacement system. Instead, this approach should be used prospectively (e.g., one estimates ahead of time when it is thought the optimum will be achieved and have a replacement system prepared to enter service at that time).

An Illustration

To illustrate our technique, we assume values of the relevant parameters. We assume a new aircraft costs $50 million with annual operating costs of $1 million in the second year. (All figures in this illustration are in real dollars.) We assume real annual operating costs increase by 3 percent per year for every year the aircraft ages. (This rate of maintenance cost growth therefore implies an annual operating cost of about $2.3 million in Year 30.)

We assume a new aircraft has a 50 percent availability rate in its first year (reflecting a break-in period), 70 percent in its second year, 90 percent in its third year, but then the availability level declines at 1 percent per year after reaching

6

the 90 percent apogee in Year 3. (This rate of availability decay implies an availability rate of about 69 percent in Year 30.)

With these assumptions, we can compute MC_t, the incremental cost per available year, for each year of aircraft age. Not surprisingly, the first year is extremely expensive—the new aircraft costs $50 million and one gets only 50 percent availability, so the cost per available year is $100 million. Subsequent years, however, are much cheaper, on the margin. In Year 2, for instance, one incurs $1 million in operating cost for 70 percent availability or $1.4 million per available year. In Year 3, the marginal cost per available year reaches its nadir at $1.1 million, but then it gradually rises as maintenance costs increase and availability rates decline. Figure 2.1 plots the real incremental cost per available year with the parameters we have assumed.

In this illustration, we have assumed, for pedagogical simplicity, that the aircraft actually flies in the year of its $50 million procurement expenditure. Our computational procedure would work equally well (although MC_1 would be infinite and hence ungraphable) if the procurement expenditure in Year 1 preceded by some number of years the first flight of the aircraft.

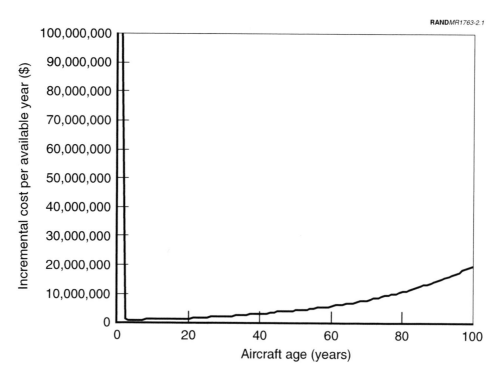

Figure 2.1—Illustrative Incremental Cost Per Available Year

Next, we calculate the annualized cost per available year *AC(N)* for each potential aircraft retirement age *N*.

Figure 2.2 shows the *AC(N)* curve (*x/y*) for our assumed parameters, including a 3.2 percent real interest rate. In this example, real annualized cost per available year is minimized at an aircraft age of 39, i.e., the optimal replacement time is when the aircraft is 39 years old.

In the next two sections, we apply our technique to the C-21A transport aircraft and the KC-135 aerial tanker.

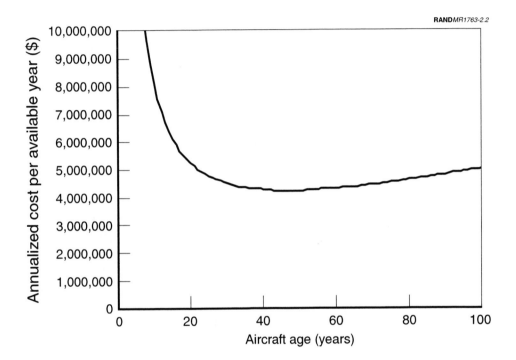

Figure 2.2—Illustrative Annualized Cost Per Available Year

8

3. The C-21A Repair Versus Replacement Decision

The C-21A and Assumptions

The C-21A is the Air Force's version of the Learjet 35 passenger aircraft, a long-range, executive transport plane. It has a crew of two pilots, can hold eight passengers with up to 1,000 pounds of luggage, and it has a flight endurance of about five hours with intercontinental range.[1] See Figure 3.1.

The first Learjet 35 flew in 1973. The Air Force accepted its current fleet of 76 C-21As between January 4, 1984 and September 25, 1987. The aircraft cost $2.8 million each in Fiscal Year (FY) 1984 dollars or about $4.3 million each in FY2002 dollars. (All dollar figures presented henceforth in this section are in FY2002 terms.)

RAND*MR1763-3.1*

Photo from *http://www.af.mil/news/factsheets/c_21A.html*.

Figure 3.1—A C-21A

---

[1]See http://abcnews.go.com/sections/us/DailyNews/stewart_learjet991026.html. Professional golfer Payne Stewart and five other people perished in an October 25, 1999 Learjet 35 crash near Aberdeen, South Dakota. See http://www.ntsb.gov/events/aberdeen/default.htm.

The C-21A has been contractor-maintained. C-21A maintenance was initially provided under a ten-year contract with a subsidiary of Learjet. Upon the expiration of that contract, the work was won by Serv-Air. Serv-Air was subsequently purchased by Raytheon before the applicable division was spun off as Raytheon Aerospace LLC.

In Figure 3.2, we show annual Air Force C-21A maintenance (fund code 3400) and modification (fund code 3010) expenditures and fleet flying hours for FY1995–2002, inclusive. These and other data in this section were provided to RAND by the C-21A program office. We do not consider military personnel, fuel, or other C-21A costs in this analysis. We did not receive such data nor do we think they vary greatly as aircraft age.

C-21A maintenance and modification expenditures have varied considerably year-to-year. The greatest expenditure variance has been in modifications with occasional large projects—for example, an FY2000 modification installing a terrain collision avoidance system on the aircraft. Meanwhile, C-21A fleet flying hours have been gradually increasing.

We also received estimates of future years' maintenance and modification costs out to 2009. It is estimated that maintenance (3400) costs will average about

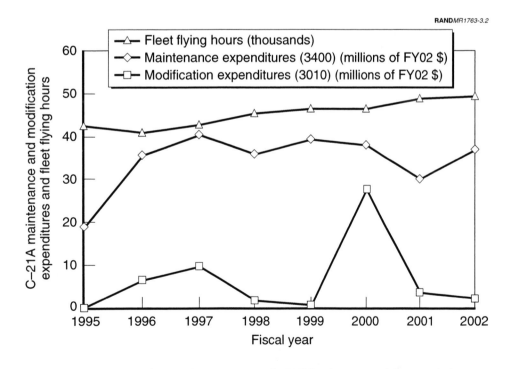

Figure 3.2—Annual C-21A Maintenance and Modification Expenditures and Fleet Flying Hours

$600,000 per aircraft per year for 2003–2009 versus the 1995–2002 annual maintenance cost average of about $450,000. Roughly speaking, this corresponds to a 3.7 percent real growth rate in annual per-aircraft maintenance expenditures. We assumed this 3.7 percent maintenance cost growth rate would continue past 2009. We assumed annual per aircraft maintenance costs over the period 1986–1994, for which we have no data, were $450,000.

We were told there were no modification (3010) costs for the C-21A prior to 1995. Modification costs are estimated to average about $60,000 per aircraft per year over 1995–2009. We assume this annual modification cost rate would hold true past 2009 with no increase in modification costs per aircraft.

We were further told that the C-21A has never had serious availability problems and that there are no reliable availability data on this aircraft. We thus ignored this issue in our analysis of the C-21A[2] and let $Availability_{It} = 1$ for all t.

Like most aircraft, the C-21A occasionally needs a fairly serious system overhaul. Air Force C-21A program personnel we talked to were particularly concerned about a 20,000 flight hour system and component replacement schedule-prescribed renovation the aircraft is slated to receive in the 2012 timeframe. This renovation will cost an estimated $500,000 per aircraft. We do not know how it will affect availability. Again, we are not considering availability issues in this section.

One challenge in this type of analysis is that we do not know what system would replace the C-21A nor at what cost. As noted, the Air Force paid $4.3 million per C-21A aircraft. However, Air Force personnel suggested its replacement would cost considerably more.

One way to estimate the replacement cost would be to add the C-21A's modification costs per aircraft into the initial acquisition cost. Roughly speaking, by 2009 the Air Force will have spent approximately $1 million per aircraft in modifications, so one might estimate the C-21A's replacement cost to be about $5.3 million per aircraft. As a rough estimate, we use this $5.3 million estimate in the calculations that follow.

Absent any other information, we assumed the C-21A would be replaced by a system that has the same maintenance and modification cost pattern, costing the same amount in inflation-adjusted dollars. We used a 3.2 percent real discount rate, in accord with 2003 OMB guidelines.

---

[2]The Air Force's Reliability and Maintainability Information System (REMIS) contains C-21A Fully Mission Capable (FMC) rate data, but the C-21A program office told us those REMIS data were not accurate for this aircraft. Indeed, the program office was not sure where REMIS was getting its C-21A FMC rates.

Bringing together our assumptions, we created Figure 3.3's depiction of the annualized cost per C-21A. The generally rising broken line is MC_I, the marginal annual cost of the C-21A; the solid horizontal line is AC_R, the minimum real annual cost of the replacement aircraft.

The 20,000 flight hour replacement schedule-prescribed renovation is portrayed as the four elevated points between 2012 and 2015, on the assumption it would take four years for it to be undertaken across all the aircraft in the fleet. After the renovation, maintenance and modification costs fall, but then the maintenance costs return to their 3.7 percent growth rate.

The lack of monotonicity in Figure 3.3's incremental cost line MC_I is noteworthy. Section 2's simple optimality condition assumed incremental cost per available year is nondecreasing past its minimum. This condition is not satisfied in Figure 3.3.

To find the solution when there is nonmonotonicity, one needs to compare the levels of annualized average expenditure for the incumbent aircraft at the two points where the upward sloping incremental cost line for the incumbent crosses the minimum annualized cost line for the replacement. In this case, the right

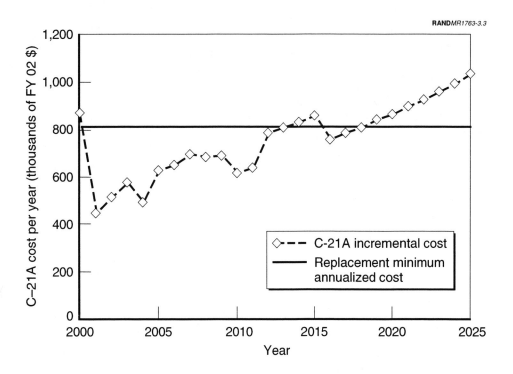

Figure 3.3—Estimated Average and Incremental Cost of C-21A Operation

crossing point in 2018 has a somewhat lower annualized average C-21A cost than the left crossing point in 2013. Hence, 2018 retirement is found to be optimal.

Uncertainty in Replacement Acquisition Cost

As noted, we do not know what sort of aircraft would replace the C-21A nor at what cost. Heretofore we assumed in the analysis that the C-21A would be replaced by an aircraft that has an acquisition cost of about $5.3 million. However, we are uncertain of this estimate.

To evaluate the effects of acquisition cost uncertainty, we analyzed a range of possible acquisition costs and the implied optimal replacement time for the C-21A, holding other parameters constant. We examined potential replacement costs from a low of $4.3 million (the inflation-adjusted C-21A acquisition cost, ignoring subsequent modifications) to a high of $10 million.[3] As one might expect, increasing the replacement's acquisition cost (but holding the replacement's annual real maintenance and modification costs equal to the C-21A's at the same age) tends to push back the optimal time to replace the C-21A. However, as shown in Figure 3.4, for most realistic replacement costs, it appears to make sense to replace the C-21A by sometime around 2020. For replacement costs less than about $5 million per aircraft, it would not make sense to undertake the 20,000 hour replacement schedule-prescribed renovation, given the other assumptions we have made.

In Figure 3.4's display, only the replacement acquisition cost is varied. We hold maintenance and modification costs constant. If the replacement aircraft also has greater maintenance and/or modification costs than the C-21A, the optimal C-21A replacement year will be pushed back.

When we discussed C-21A replacement with Air Mobility Command personnel, they suggested they might replace the C-21A with a larger, more capable aircraft.

There are several ways one might address such a possibility in this modeling framework. First, if the 76 C-21As could be replaced by fewer "C-21Bs," one should use a proportional scaling factor. If, for example, 50 larger C-21Bs could do the same work as the 76 C-21As, one could scale all C-21B expenses per aircraft down by 50/76 to put those C-21B expenses in "C-21A equivalent" terms.

---

[3]Phelps (2002) indicates that the new Learjet 40 has a retail price of $6.75 million. Of course, we do not know whether the Air Force would consider this aircraft to be an adequate replacement for the C-21A.

We have also ignored the issue of potential re-sale value of the existing C-21As. If they could be sold into the private sector, this would reduce the net cost of the aircraft's replacement.

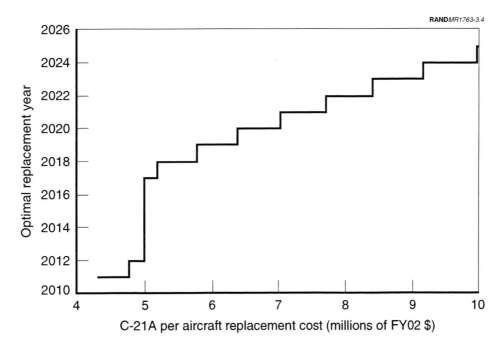

**Figure 3.4—Optimal C-21A Replacement Year as a Function of Replacement
Acquisition Cost**

Second, if one wished to replace C-21As with the same number of more capable
C-21Bs, one needs to adjust C-21B acquisition, maintenance, and modification
costs downward to reflect their increased capability (or, symmetrically, scale up
C-21A maintenance and modification costs). Without such a replacement cost
adjustment, this repair-replace analysis tool would be inappropriately averse to
calling for replacement of the existing system.

4. Estimating Model Parameters for the KC-135

We next apply our analysis technique to the KC-135 tanker.

Between 1954 and 1965, the Air Force purchased 732 KC-135A in-flight refueling aircraft from Boeing. The KC-135A is similar to Boeing's 707 commercial passenger aircraft. See Pike (2002).

Since they were purchased, the KC-135s have undergone a series of modifications. Those given refurbished Pratt and Whitney JT3D engines were relabeled KC-135Es. Figure 4.1 displays a KC-135E.

Later, 410 KC-135s (some KC-135Es, some KC-135As) were given new CFM56 engines, produced by CFM International, resulting in better fuel efficiency and less noise. See Department of the Air Force (2001). This re-engine process began in 1984 and is ongoing. CFM International is a joint venture between SNECMA Moteurs of France and General Electric. See CFM International (2002). KC-135s with the CFM56 engine were labeled KC-135Rs. Figure 4.2 displays a KC-135R.

Photo courtesy of Brian Lockett of the Goleta Air and Space Museum, at *http://www.air-and-space.com/200002%20red%20flag%20b.htm.*

Figure 4.1—A KC-135E

Photo courtesy of John Pike of GlobalSecurity.org (*http://www.globalsecurity.org/military/systems/ aircraft/kc-135r-pics.htm*).

Figure 4.2—A KC-135R

Fifty-six aircraft, designated KC-135Q, were fitted with special navigation and communications equipment to refuel and support the SR-71 Blackbird, a high-speed, high-altitude reconnaissance aircraft. See Aerospaceweb.org (2001). Later, these KC-135Qs received the same CFM56 engines as the KC-135R and were relabeled the KC-135T. Since the Air Force no longer uses the SR-71, the KC-135R and KC-135T are now, in large part, identical from a mission perspective. KC-135s can carry approximately 200,000 pounds of fuel.

The Air Force no longer flies any KC-135As; all remaining tankers either have the JT3D or CFM56 engine. The last KC-135A flight hours were in July 1994, according to the Air Force's Reliability and Maintainability Information System (REMIS).

KC-135 Availability

Unlike in the C-21A case, we can consider KC-135 availability patterns in our analysis.

In Figures 4.3–4.5, we show the monthly availability rates of the three remaining KC-135 variants from January 1995 to September 2002. These data come from REMIS. An aircraft is said to be Fully Mission Capable (FMC) if it can perform all its missions. An aircraft is Partially Mission Capable if it can fly safely with

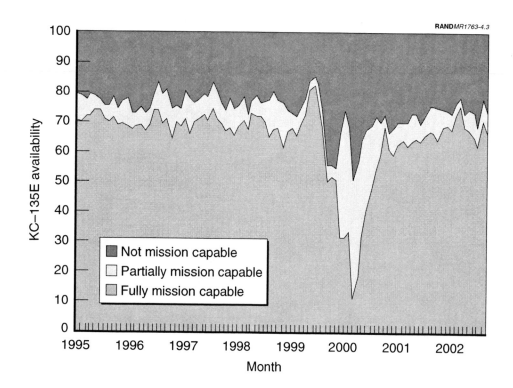

Figure 4.3—KC-135E Monthly Availability

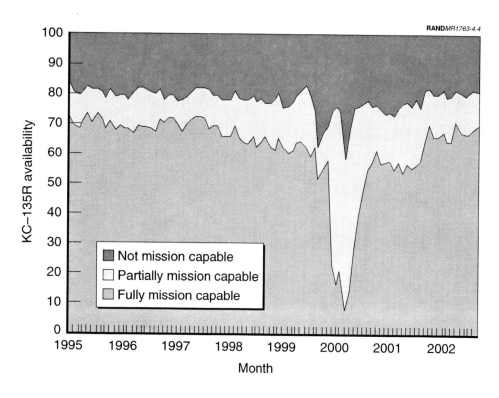

Figure 4.4—KC-135R Monthly Availability

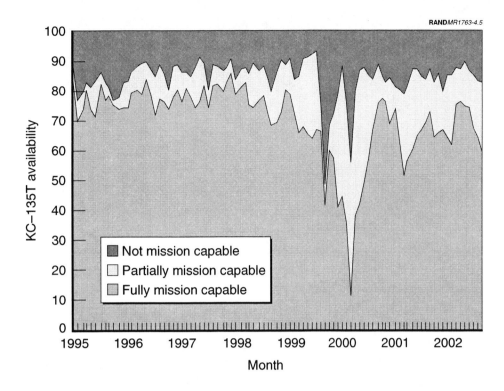

Figure 4.5—KC-135T Monthly Availability

appropriate restrictions, but some of its capabilities are not functioning correctly. (For example, an aircraft might still fly during daylight hours even if its night-vision equipment is not working.) A Not Mission Capable aircraft cannot safely perform its missions.

Most striking in Figures 4.3–4.5 is the sharp decline in KC-135 availability in 1999 and 2000. There was a fatal KC-135E crash in Germany in January 1999 that is now believed to have been caused by horizontal stabilizer trim actuator problems. See *Air Force News* (1999). In the period following that crash, a series of flight restrictions were imposed on KC-135s, resulting in a sharp downturn in the aircraft's FMC status. The entire fleet of KC-135s was carefully inspected, including a February 2000 standdown of part of the fleet to look for other potential problems in the stabilizer portion of the tail section. The Air Force believes it has now addressed this problem.

One could replot Figures 4.3–4.5 using aircraft system average age on the horizontal axis, not calendar month. The portrayals would not be meaningfully different from Figures 4.3–4.5, however.

In Table 4.1, we describe the three KC-135 fleets in January 1995 and January 2002. The three fleets have aged approximately linearly over the last seven years.

Table 4.1

KC-135 Fleet Age Trends
(years)

		KC-135E	KC-135R	KC-135T
January 1995	Possessed aircraft	138	291	28
	Computed average age[a]	35.7	33.1	34.8
January 2002	Possessed aircraft	102	301	45
	Computed average age	42.8	40.2	42.0

[a]Computed average age is measured from the date the Air Force accepted each airplane from its manufacturer.

The number of KC-135Es has fallen, in part because the Air Force converted 24 KC-135Es into KC-135Rs by giving them CFM56 engines. The number of KC-135Ts was larger in January 2002 than in January 1995, but not because the Air Force bought any new KC-135Ts. Instead, some KC-135Ts that were in the depot system in January 1995 were not in January 2002, so they tallied as "possessed" in January 2002, but not in January 1995.[1]

If one wishes to estimate how KC-135 availability has varied with system age, the key analytical issue is how to handle the 1999–2000 availability trough. Was it an idiosyncratic episode that should not be considered in estimating the KC-135 availability time trend? Or was it exactly the sort of incident that will become increasingly common as this system ages?

In Figure 4.6, we plot the monthly KC-135E FMC rate as a function of average aircraft age, e.g., $FMC = kx^{Age}$ or $\ln(FMC) = \ln(k) + Age * \ln(x)$. We also include two regression lines. The lower, thicker line ("All data regression") suggests the KC-135E FMC rate is declining at about 3.2 percent per year as the system ages. The upper, thinner line ("Remove outliers regression") suggests that KC-135E FMC rate has declined at about half the full data-estimated rate (1.6 percent) as the system has aged. The upper line's regression excludes December 1999 through May 2000 from the regression estimation; the lower line does not.

We ran similar estimations for the KC-135R and KC-135T. Their all/no outliers FMC decline rates were 4.0 percent/2.3 percent (KC-135R) and 3.9 percent/2.8 percent (KC-135T).[2] Table 4.2 presents our FMC trend regression results.

---

[1]Possessed aircraft are those held by Air Combat Command, U.S. Air Forces in Europe, Air Education and Training Command, Air Force Reserve, Air Mobility Command, Air National Guard, Pacific Air Forces, or Special Operations Command for at least a portion of the month. Most notably, an aircraft does not count as possessed if it is currently undergoing depot-level maintenance or modification.

[2]These decline rate estimates are derived by exponentiating Table 4.2's age coefficients, e.g., $e^{-.041} = .960$ for a 4.0 percent decline rate.

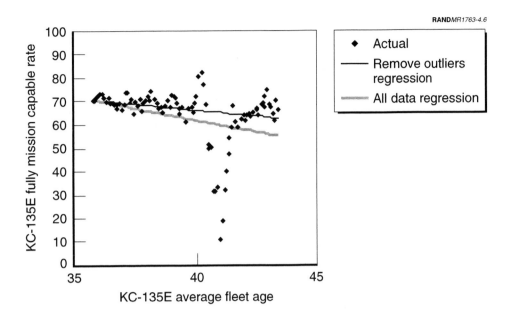

Figure 4.6—KC-135E Fully Mission Capable Rate as a Function of Average System Age

Table 4.2

KC-135 Natural Log of Fully Mission Capable Rate Regressions

	KC-135E		KC-135R		KC-135T	
	All Data	No Outliers	All Data	No Outliers	All Data	No Outliers
Observations	93	87	93	87	93	87
R-squared	0.066	0.118	0.068	0.252	0.121	0.273
Intercept coefficient estimate	5.415	4.820	5.603	5.007	5.776	5.387
Intercept estimate standard error	0.504	0.184	0.591	0.157	0.439	0.197
Intercept T statistic	10.751	26.252	9.484	31.879	13.152	27.335
Intercept P value	0.000	0.000	0.000	0.000	0.000	0.000
Age coefficient estimate	−0.032	−0.016	−0.041	−0.023	−0.040	−0.029
Age estimate standard error	0.013	0.005	0.016	0.004	0.011	0.005
Age T statistic	−2.541	−3.371	−2.578	−5.353	−3.540	−5.656
Age P value	0.013	0.001	0.012	0.000	0.001	0.000

Our instinct is to remove the availability trough from the data and thereby assert the more optimistic availability decline pattern. Other informed observers may feel differently.

20

KC-135 Maintenance Costs

REMIS also provides data for installation-level on- and off-equipment maintenance hours. On-equipment maintenance is maintenance accomplished on a complete end item, i.e., work on the actual aircraft. Off-equipment maintenance is work performed on broken parts removed from an aircraft, often at an intermediate-level maintenance facility. See Air Force Instruction 21-129, May 1, 1998 (United States Air Force, 1998).

In Figures 4.7–4.9, we show the time trend in total maintenance hours for the three KC-135 variants.

In Figures 4.10–4.12, we sum the monthly data on on- and off-equipment maintenance hours and normalize them by the number of possessed aircraft and plot them against average fleet age. All three KC-135 variants show increasing on- and off-equipment maintenance hours per possessed aircraft.

Figures 4.10–4.12 also show best-fit regression lines of how aircraft age appears to affect maintenance hours per possessed aircraft. We assume a model of the form

$$Cost = kx^{Age} \text{ or } \ln(Cost) = \ln(k) + Age * \ln(x)$$

where $Cost$ = monthly average number of maintenance hours per possessed aircraft and Age = aircraft average age. The Age coefficient estimate $\ln(x)$ can then

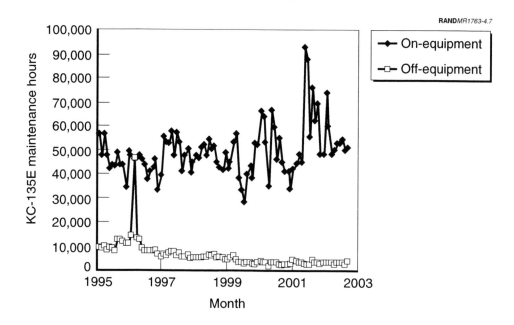

Figure 4.7—KC-135E Monthly On- and Off-Equipment Maintenance Hours

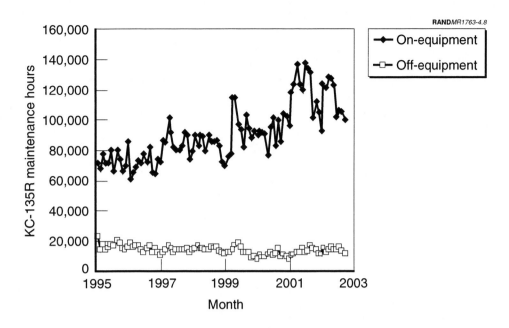

Figure 4.8—KC-135R Monthly On- and Off-Equipment Maintenance Hours

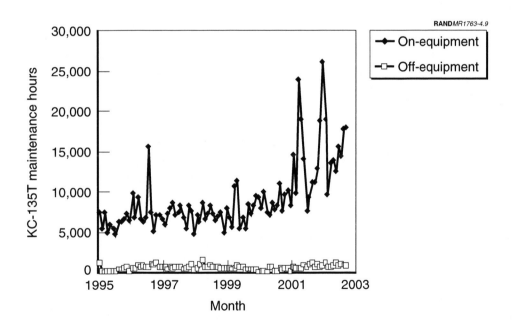

Figure 4.9—KC-135T Monthly On- and Off-Equipment Maintenance Hours

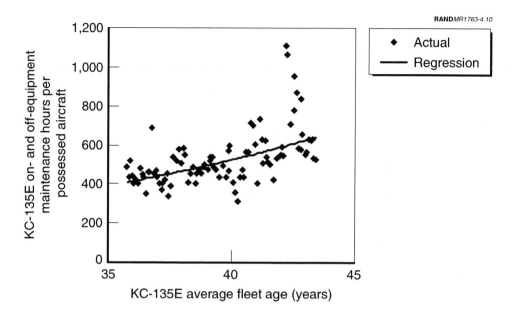

Figure 4.10—KC-135E Monthly On- and Off-Equipment Maintenance Hours Per Possessed Aircraft

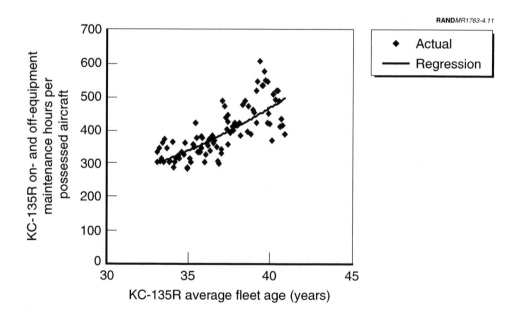

Figure 4.11—KC-135R Monthly On- and Off-Equipment Maintenance Hours Per Possessed Aircraft

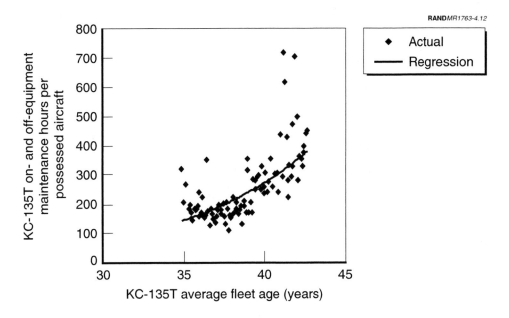

Figure 4.12—KC-135T Monthly On- and Off-Equipment Maintenance Hours Per Possessed Aircraft

be exponentiated to derive the implied age-driven cost growth rate. As discussed below, a fuller cost model could include other independent variables beyond age.

As indicated in Table 4.3, all three systems show statistically significant age effects in on- and off-equipment maintenance per possessed aircraft.

Table 4.3

KC-135 Natural Log of On- and Off-Equipment Maintenance Hour Per Possessed Aircraft Regressions

	KC-135E	KC-135R	KC-135T
Observations	93	93	93
R-squared	0.331	0.607	0.503
Intercept coefficient estimate	3.913	3.579	0.596
Intercept estimate standard error	0.348	0.201	0.507
Intercept T statistic	11.248	17.840	1.176
Intercept P value	0.000	0.000	0.243
Age coefficient estimate	0.059	0.064	0.126
Age estimate standard error	0.009	0.005	0.013
Age T statistic	6.707	11.857	9.600
Age P value	0.000	0.000	0.000

The Age coefficient estimates in Table 4.3 imply age-driven maintenance hour per possessed aircraft annual compound growth rates of 6.06 percent for the KC-135E, 6.64 percent for the KC-135R, and 13.38 percent for the KC-135T.

We caution against overinterpretation of these empirical estimates. Many factors in the Air Force—such as basing patterns, workforce skill and experience mixes, deployments, and maintenance policies—change over time. Hence, point estimates such as Table 4.3's age coefficients may embody a number of factors beyond aging effects, as traditionally defined.

Setting Up Maintenance Regressions

In Table 4.3's regressions (superimposed on Figures 4.10–4.12), we used a very simple structure where the natural log of monthly maintenance hours per aircraft was regressed on a constant term and that month's average fleet age.

There are, however, numerous other approaches one might consider. Pyles (2003) experiments with more linear estimations, e.g., $Cost = a + b * Age$. While it is often difficult to choose between compound and linear approaches, they give very different predictions for more distant periods. Pyles (2003) finds evidence for the greater out-year growth implicit in compound models only for heavy structural maintenance. Most other maintenance categories (e.g., on-equipment maintenance) showed more linear growth, with some material consumption categories leveling off after 20 to 30 years.

An additional issue is how and whether to include flying hours in estimations. It is common in the literature to use maintenance hours or costs per flying hour as the dependent variable and regress this ratio on system age or time. See, for instance, Stoll and Davis (1993), Johnson (1993), Ramsey, French, and Sperry (1998), and Jondrow et al. (2002).

We were reluctant to do so. In Keating and Camm (2002), we demonstrated there is little short-run empirical relationship between depot-level expenditures and flying hours. For this reason, depot maintenance hours per flying hour tend to decline if monthly flying hours increase. Hence, with the recent upturn in aircraft usage due to operations in Afghanistan and Iraq, a regression of depot maintenance hours per flying hour on age may find an artificially small, if not negative, age effect.

Using an impressively large Navy and Marine F/A-18C data set, Francis and Shaw (2000) regress aircraft-specific total monthly maintenance hours on age, deployment status, monthly flight hours, and other variables. They find a considerable impact of aircraft age on maintenance hours. They note that it would be valuable to try to disentangle cumulative flight-hour effects from age effects. Such a cumulative utilization versus calendar age exploration would be particularly relevant to the KC-135 in that the KC-135 fleet is aged but has relatively few flight hours. See United States General Accounting Office (2002).

Hildebrandt and Sze (1990) used operating and support costs per aircraft as their dependent variable, but they used a cross-sectional regression approach with multiple weapon systems' data in a pooled estimation. In Appendix B of Keating and Camm (2002), we argued such cross-system analysis can give spurious results.

Jackson, Mitchell, and Ott (2002) analyze depot-level reparable and operating and support costs per aircraft. The Congressional Budget Office (2001) presents both per operating hour and per aircraft data.

It could be a paper unto itself to explore different functional forms and independent variables. Along with age and flying hours, one might think variables such as number of takeoffs and landings and where the aircraft has operated (e.g., humid versus dry areas) could be relevant.

For our pedagogical purposes here, we will be content to note these possible extensions, any of which could be employed using our approach.

Depot-Level Maintenance

In addition to installation-level on- and off-equipment maintenance, every 60–66 months an aircraft is to receive Programmed Depot Maintenance (PDM). PDM involves more complicated work than on- and off-equipment maintenance—e.g., intensive corrosion, metal cracking, leak, and wire chafing inspection and repair—and requires sophisticated equipment and more highly skilled labor not typically found at the installations where aircraft are ordinarily based.

This work takes place at three large depots the Air Force owns at Hill Air Force Base, Ogden, Utah; Robins Air Force Base, Warner Robins, Georgia; and Tinker Air Force Base near Oklahoma City, Oklahoma. Some PDM work is also performed at other locations, such as the now-privatized facility at what was Kelly Air Force Base in San Antonio, Texas.

The actual PDM work done varies with, for instance, the condition of the specific aircraft. However, there is a standard depot maintenance package. In Figure

4.13 and Table 4.4, we show that the standard KC-135 PDM package has been growing at an estimated 7.62 percent ($e^{.073}$) annual rate as the aircraft has aged.[3]

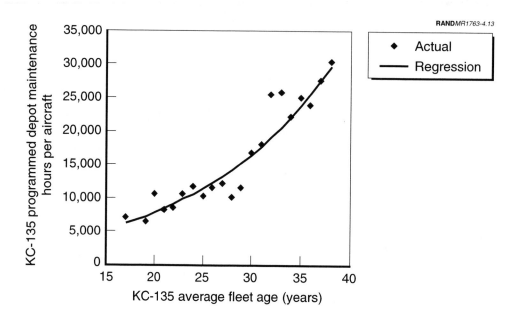

Figure 4.13—KC-135 PDM Hours

Table 4.4

**KC-135 Natural Log of Programmed Depot Maintenance
Hours Per Aircraft Regression**

Observations	21
R-squared	0.895
Intercept coefficient estimate	7.509
Intercept estimate standard error	0.165
Intercept T statistic	45.552
Intercept P value	0.000
Age coefficient estimate	0.073
Age estimate standard error	0.006
Age T statistic	12.750
Age P value	0.000

---

[3]These PDM data do not distinguish among KC-135Es, Rs, and Ts.

Implementing the Model in Section 2

The remaining important parameters to input into a model such as that described in Section 2 are the incremental annual sustainment costs of a current KC-135 and the acquisition and sustainment costs of a new, replacement aircraft.

Data provided by RAND colleague Michael Kennedy suggest that total sustainment costs per KC-135 aircraft have averaged roughly $3.53 million per year. (The cost data presented in this section are in constant FY2000 terms.) See Table 4.5.

Table 4.5's sustainment cost categories are somewhat different from the categorization we have used heretofore. However, in order to apply our model, we had to make assumptions about how each category grows as aircraft age. Our assumptions are shown in the right column of the table.

We assume operating personnel and support costs and contract maintenance costs do not grow as aircraft age.

Borrowing an estimate from Stoll and Davis (1993), we assume fuel usage per aircraft grows at 0.6 percent annual rate.

We assume reparable costs grow at a 3.5 percent annual rate, in accord with findings of our colleague Gregory Hildebrandt.

Organizational maintenance is akin to on- and off-equipment maintenance whereas aircraft overhaul is akin to PDM. Hence, we assume organizational

Table 4.5

Annual Sustainment Costs of the KC-135 Fleet in FY2000
(per aircraft)

Category	Millions FY00$/Tail	Assumed Growth Rate (percent)
Operating personnel and support	1.04	0
Contract maintenance	0.01	0
Fuel	0.42	0.6
Reparables	0.19	3.5
Organizational maintenance	0.80	6.64
Aircraft overhaul	0.55	7.62
Engine overhaul	0.02	Pattern found in Pyles (2003)
Modifications	0.50	2.1
Total	3.53	

maintenance grows at a 6.64 percent annual rate, in accord with Table 4.3's KC-135R estimate. We assume aircraft overhaul costs grow at a 7.62 percent rate, in accord with Table 4.4.

Both our organizational maintenance and aircraft overhaul cost assumptions are subject to controversy. Both Table 4.3's and Table 4.4's data are in hours, not costs. If there were excess capacity in the organizational maintenance or depot systems, repair or overhaul hours could increase without costs increasing commensurably. Another possibility is that hours are growing but material usage is not, so that total costs would not grow as quickly as hours. (In Table 4.7 below, we loosen our maintenance and overhaul cost growth-rate assumptions.)

Pyles (2003) analyzes the empirical relationship between engine overhaul costs and various covariates, including aircraft age. We use his Table 5.26 regression results to estimate how KC-135 engine overhaul costs will grow as the aircraft ages further.

We assume modification costs are growing at a 2.1 percent rate (for logical consistency reasons discussed below in footnote 4).

We assume KC-135 availability will continue to decline at a 2.3 percent rate, Table 4.2's KC-135R estimate, omitting the availability trough.

Following Kennedy et al.'s unpublished RAND research, we assume that the KC-135 will be replaced by a variation of the Boeing 767 (although this analysis is not intended to endorse the 767 over, for instance, an Airbus alternative). Borrowing Kennedy et al.'s parameters, we assume a 767 tanker variant would cost $151.3 million. A 767 would have considerably lower sustainment costs than a KC-135, as shown in Table 4.6.

Kirkpatrick (2000) notes that the actual life cycle cost of a particular system cannot be finally determined until after it has been withdrawn from service. In contrast, in this exercise, we must step far into the speculative range by estimating the entire life cycle cost of a weapon system that is not yet operated by the U.S. Air Force. Ultimately, one needs to make some guess as to the life cycle cost of the 767 (or any KC-135 replacement) in order to assess when it is optimal to retire the KC-135. (There are data on the maintenance history of 767 passenger aircraft, but a tanker version has not been widely used heretofore.)

As with the KC-135, we assume 767 operating personnel and support and contract maintenance costs will not grow as the aircraft age. We also use the 0.6 percent annual fuel-growth estimate and the 3.5 percent reparables growth-rate estimate.

Table 4.6

Annual Sustainment Costs of the KC-135 Versus 767 Fleet
(per aircraft)

Category	KC-135 Millions FY00$/Tail	767 Millions FY00$/Tail	767 Assumed Growth Rate (percent)
Operating personnel and support	1.04	0.91	0
Contract maintenance	0.01	0.04	0
Fuel	0.42	0.40	0.6
Reparables	0.19	0.08	3.5
Organizational maintenance	0.80	0.68	0 for first 15 years, 2 for next 15, 6.64 thereafter
Aircraft overhaul	0.55	0.13	0 for first 15 years, 2 for next 15, 7.62 thereafter
Engine overhaul	0.02	0.01	0 for first 20 years, 3.5 for next 20, follows Pyles' pattern thereafter
Modifications	0.50	0.30	0 for first 15 years, 2.1 thereafter
Total	3.53	2.55	

Table 4.3's organizational maintenance cost-growth estimates are too large to plausibly hold over the life of the aircraft. Instead, we assume 767 organizational maintenance costs would be constant (in real terms) for the first 15 years of operation, grow at 2 percent per year for the next 15, then grow at 6.64 percent (like Table 4.3's KC-135R estimate) thereafter.

We similarly assume aircraft overhaul costs are constant for the first 15 years, grow at 2 percent per year for the next 15, then grow at 7.62 percent (as in Table 4.4) thereafter.

We assume engine overhaul costs are static for the first 20 years, then grow at 3.5 percent per year, thereby equaling the KC-135 engine overhaul costs at age 40. Thereafter, we assert they follow the Pyles' KC-135 engine overhaul pattern.

We assume annual modification costs would be static for the first 15 years of 767 tanker operation, then grow at roughly 2.1 percent per year (thereby matching the KC-135's $500,000 in modification costs per aircraft at age 40).[4]

---

[4]Pyles (2003) finds no tendency for modifications to increase as aircraft age. However, in Table 4.6, we assume a KC-135 has a greater annual modification cost than a new 767. Hence, logically, it would seem as if some sort of increasing modification rate must be assumed. A 2.1 percent rate was chosen because, if it started after 15 years of static 767 modifications, it would bring the annual 767 modification rate to the KC-135 level when the 767 reaches the KC-135's age.

We assume the aircraft would have 90 percent availability during its first 15 years, 85 percent the next 15, and then decline at 2.3 percent (like the KC-135R) per year thereafter.

A further important advantage for the newer 767 aircraft is that the Air Force could replace KC-135s on a more favorable basis than one-for-one. In our analysis, we assume 100 767 tankers could replace 136 KC-135s because of availability, capacity, and capability improvements in the 767. Hence, for computational purposes, we can scale down all 767 acquisition and maintenance costs by the factor 100/136 to put its costs in "KC-135 equivalent" terms. (For example, the "KC-135 equivalent" acquisition cost of a 767 is therefore about $111 million.)

With these 767 tanker parameters, we find that it would be optimal for the Air Force to operate the 767 for 47 years with AC_R equal to $7.91 million per year (in "KC-135 equivalent" terms). With KC-135 expenses growing and availability declining, as we have computed, it is then computed to be optimal to replace the KC-135 after its 47th year of operation or in 2008. (The finding that it is optimal to operate both the KC-135s and 767 tankers for 47 years is a coincidence.) In Year 48 (2009), we estimate there would be about $4.71 million in KC-135 expenditures per aircraft for 58 percent availability, so the cost per available year (MC_I) of $8.08 million would exceed the 767 lifetime average cost per available year (AC_R). See Figure 4.14.

Given the myriad parameters in our modeling exercise, a full robustness analysis could be its own paper. For our illustrative purposes, we restrict ourselves to a few extensions.

In Figure 4.14, we assume 100 767 tankers could replace 136 KC-135s. There is, however, considerable uncertainty as to this replacement ratio. Daniels (2002) speaks of a 100/126 ratio; the GAO (2002) uses 100/127. In Figure 4.15, we relax our replacement ratio assumption. The horizontal axis is the number of KC-135s that could be replaced by 100 767s, ranging from a low of 100 up to 136. On the vertical axis, we plot our computed optimal KC-135 replacement age. As one expects, a less favorable 767/KC-135 replacement ratio pushes back the optimal time to retire the KC-135s. That said, KC-135 replacement is still recommended in the next ten years, even with a less favorable replacement ratio.

Another excursion we undertook was to ignore all aircraft availability issues, i.e., let $Availability_t = 1$ for all t for both the KC-135 and 767. Under this excursion, one would minimize total cost but ignore availability differences over time. In

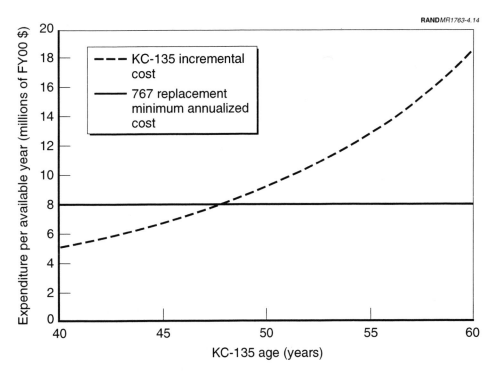

Figure 4.14—KC-135 Projected Expenditures Per Available Year

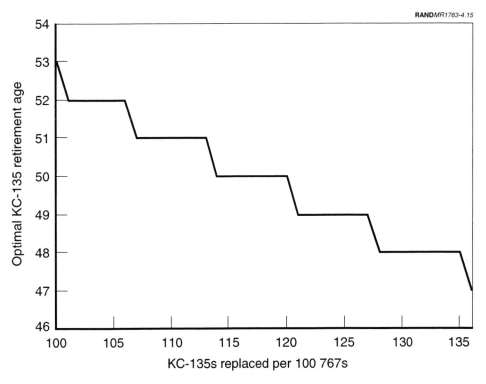

Figure 4.15—KC-135 Optimal Replacement Age as a Function of KC-135/767 Replacement Ratio

this case, the optimal KC-135 retirement age is 55 (2016), increased from 47. It is not surprising that one would keep an aging system longer if one is not concerned about declining aircraft availability.

We next explore which other KC-135 parameters would have to vary to change our broad policy conclusion that the fleet should be retired relatively soon. As shown in Table 4.7, it would take a confluence of positive events (e.g., no further organizational maintenance or aircraft overhaul cost growth and no further availability decline) for it to be optimal to keep the KC-135 fleet flying much past 2015 or so. In Case C, we have the KC-135's availability not declining further, but there is still consideration given for increased availability with a new 767.

Table 4.7

KC-135 Parameter Exploration

Case	Optimal KC-135 Retirement Age	Year
Baseline	47	2008
A. Organizational maintenance costs not growing (0% versus +6.64%)	50	2011
B. Aircraft overhaul costs not growing (0% versus +7.62%)	49	2010
C. Availability not declining (0% versus –2.3%)	51	2012
A & B	54	2015
A & C	56	2017
B & C	56	2017
A & B & C	77	2038

5. Conclusions

In this report, we have sketched a procedure for determining when it is optimal to replace, rather than repair, an existing aircraft fleet. We then applied that procedure to the cases of the C-21A and KC-135 aircraft.

Building upon the work of Greenfield and Persselin (2002), we presented a relatively simple optimality condition. Specifically, it is optimal to operate another year if and only if the incremental cost per available year is less than the lifetime average cost per available year that would be associated with a new aircraft. This optimality condition assumes that incremental costs per available year are nondecreasing. In reality, this monotonicity condition may not be satisfied.

However, in Section 3, we present C-21A data where incremental costs are not monotonic but where one can nevertheless fairly easily find the optimal solution. Based on our extrapolation and analysis of data we received from the Air Force's C-21A program office, we find it would be optimal to replace the C-21A in the 2020 timeframe.

In Section 4, we analyzed the KC-135 tanker. Data suggest the KC-135 has had both worsening availability and increasing maintenance costs in recent years. We then combined our estimated aging effects with data on KC-135 operating and support costs as provided by our colleague Michael Kennedy. These data were then juxtaposed with estimates of the acquisition and operating costs of the 767 tanker, a potential replacement for the KC-135.

Our finding was that it appears to be optimal to replace the KC-135 by the end of the decade, assuming KC-135 maintenance costs and availability continue to worsen on their current trajectory. Of course, with the natural lags in acquiring new aircraft, action would need to be taken in the relatively near term to implement this recommendation.

Both our C-21A and KC-135 findings are only suggestive; we undertook these analyses solely to illustrate the capabilities of our modeling approach. Deeper inquiry into these aircraft's replacement decisions would be appropriate.

We think the tool we have developed could be usefully applied to other systems' repair-versus-replace decisions.

References

ABCNews.com, "The Learjet 35: Aircraft Popular with Corporate Execs" (http://abcnews.go.com/sections/us/DailyNews/stewart_learjet991026.html), October 26, 1999.

Aerospaceweb.org, *Boeing, C-135 Stratolifter, KC-135 Stratotanker, Cargo Transport, Refueling Tanker* (http://www.aerospaceweb.org/aircraft/transport-m/c135/index.shtml), May 2001.

Air Force News, "Air Force releases KC-135 accident report" (http://www.af.mil/news/Jun1999/n19990607_991115.html), June 7, 1999.

CFM International, *USAF Expands CFM56-2-Powered RC-135 Fleet* (http://www.cfm56.com/news/press/cfm02-18.htm), July 22, 2002.

Congressional Budget Office, *The Effects of Aging on the Costs of Operating and Maintaining Military Equipment*, August 2001.

Daniels, Mitchell E., Memo to Senator John McCain, Office of Management and Budget, May 3, 2002.

Department of the Air Force, *Fact Sheet: KC-135 Stratotanker* (http://www.af.mil/news/factsheets/KC_135_Stratotanker.html), July 2001.

Department of the Air Force, *Fact Sheet: C-21A* (http://www.af.mil/news/factsheets/C_21A.html), February 2002.

Francis, Peter, and Geoff Shaw, *Effect of Aircraft Age on Maintenance Costs*, Alexandria, VA: Center for Naval Analyses, 2000.

Goleta Air and Space Museum, available at http://www.air-and-space.com/200002%20red%20flag%20b.htm.

Graham, Bradley, "Air Force Lease With Boeing Still Under Fire," *Washington Post*, July 7, 2003, p. A02.

Greenfield, Victoria A., and David M. Persselin, *An Economic Framework for Evaluating Military Aircraft Replacement*, Santa Monica, CA: RAND, MR-1489-AF, 2002.

Hildebrandt, Gregory G., and Man-Bing Sze, *An Estimation of USAF Aircraft Operating and Support Cost Relations*, Santa Monica, CA: RAND, N-3062-ACQ, 1990.

Jackson, A. C. , T. J. Mitchell, and L. M. Ott, *Identification of Operations and Support Cost and Availability Drivers*, Marietta, GA: Lockheed Martin Aeronautics Company, AFRL-VA-WP-TR-2002, September 2002.

Johnson, John A., *Age Impacts on Operating and Support Costs: Navy Aircraft Age Analysis Methodology*, Patuxent River, MD: Naval Aviation Maintenance Office Logistics Engineering Department, Resource Analysis Division, August 1993.

Jondrow, James M., et al., *Age Cost Model*, Alexandria, VA: Center for Naval Analyses, D0000432.A1/SR1, July 2001.

Jondrow, James M., Robert P. Trost, Michael Ye, John P. Hall, Rebecca L. Kirk, Laura J. Junor, Peter J. Francis, Geoffrey B. Shaw, Darlene E. Stafford, and Barbara H. Measell, *Support Costs and Aging Aircraft: Implications for Budgeting and Procurement*, Alexandria, VA: Center for Naval Analyses, CAB D0004621.A2/Final, January 2002.

Keating, Edward G., and Frank Camm, *How Should the U.S. Air Force Depot Maintenance Activity Group Be Funded?: Insights from Expenditure and Flying Hour Data*, Santa Monica, CA: RAND, MR-1487-AF, 2002.

Kennedy, Michael, Gregory Hildebrandt, and Man-Bing Sze, "Common Replacement Asset (CRA) Study Results Briefing," unpublished RAND research.

Kirkpatrick, David L. I., "Life Cycle Costs for Decision Support—A Study of the Various Life Cycle Costs Used at Different Levels of Defence Policy and Management," *Defence and Peace Economics*, 11 (4), pp. 333–368, 2000.

National Transportation Safety Board, "Learjet 35, Aberdeen, South Dakota, October 25, 1999," DCA00MA005 (http://www.ntsb.gov/events/aberdeen/default.htm).

Office of Management and Budget, "OMB Circular No. A-94, Appendix C, Discount Rates for Cost-Effectiveness, Lease Purchase, and Related Analyses" (http://www.whitehouse.gov/omb/circulars/a094/a94_appx-c.html), January 2003.

Phelps, Mark. "Bombardier Launches Two Learjet Siblings," *Aviation International News* (http://www.ainonline.com/Publications/farn/farn_02/farn_02d1_bombardierpg1.html), July 22–28, 2002.

Pike, John, "KC-135 Stratotanker," *GlobalSecurity.org* (http://www.globalsecurity.org/military/systems/aircraft/kc-135.htm), February 2002.

Pyles, Raymond A., *Aging Aircraft: USAF Workload and Material Consumption Life Cycle Patterns*, Santa Monica, CA: RAND, MR-1641-AF, 2003.

Ramsey, Tom, Carl French, and Kenneth R. Sperry, "Airframe Maintenance Trend Analysis" briefing, Oklahoma City Air Logistics Center (Ramsey) and The Boeing Company (French and Sperry), 1998.

Squeo, Anne Marie, and J. Lynn Lunsford, "Boeing Cuts Its Proposed Price to Lease Jetliners to Air Force," *The Wall Street Journal*, May 23, 2003, p. A2.

Stoll, Laurence, and Stan Davis, *Aircraft Age Impact on Individual Operating and Support Cost Elements*, Patuxent River, MD: Naval Aviation Maintenance

Office Logistics Engineering Department, Resource Analysis Division, July 1993.

Svitak, Amy, and Gail Kaufman, "Rumsfeld Presses for Analysis of Plan to Lease Boeing 767s," *Air Force Times*, February 17, 2003, p. 23.

United States Air Force, *Two Level Maintenance and Regional Repair of Air Force Weapon Systems and Equipment*, Air Force Instruction 21-191 (http://www.e-publishing.af.mil/pubfiles/af/21/afi21-129/afi21-129.pdf), May 1, 1998.

United States General Accounting Office (GAO), *Air Force Aircraft: Preliminary Information on Air Force Tanker Leasing*, GAO-02-724R, May 2002.